Let's Learn Hiragana

Let's
Learn
Hiragana

Yasuko Kosaka Mitamura

KODANSHA INTERNATIONAL
Tokyo • New York • London

Distributed in the United States by Kodansha America, Inc., 575 Lexington Avenue, New York, N.Y. 10022, and in the United Kingdom and continental Europe by Kodansha Europe Ltd., Tavern Quay, Rope Street, London SE16 7TX.

Published by Kodansha International Ltd., 17-14 Otowa 1-chome, Bunkyo-ku, Tokyo 112-8652, and Kodansha America, Inc.

ISBN 0-87011-709-2
ISBN 4-7700-1209-8 (in Japan)
LCC 84-82275

First edition, 1985
03 04 05 06 07 08 09 10   25 24 23 22 21 20 19

www.thejapanpage.com

Contents

PREFACE

The Japanese writing system is so different from the English alphabet that written Japanese may seem to be more complicated than it really is. Actually, Hiragana symbols, which comprise the basis of Japanese writing, are not difficult to learn. By using this workbook as a study guide, the student should be able to learn all the Hiragana symbols easily, in a relatively short time.

This workbook is specially designed and organized so that the beginning student, who is studying Japanese as a foreign language, can learn Hiragana through self-study, without the aid of an instructor. Each section contains sufficient explanation and exercises to enable students to study and practice on their own until proficiency has been attained. Consequently, the use of this workbook will eliminate the need for extensive writing drills in class. The class time can then be utilized more effectively for matters that require the presence of an instructor, such as question-and-answer type oral drills.

This book is composed of four chapters: chapter 1 introduces the forty-six basic Hiragana and the sixty-one modified symbols which are derived from them. Chapter 2 explains how to write words using Hiragana symbols. Chapter 3 shows how to write sentences, and chapter 4 contains review exercises. The derivation of Hiragana is presented in Appendix B.

In learning any foreign language, it is important to place equal emphasis on the four skills: hearing, speaking, reading and writing. Therefore, it is an essential prerequisite to become very familiar with Hiragana for the eventual mastery of Japanese. The student will find that diligent use of this workbook will be of great benefit in the quest for proficiency in Japanese.

Throughout this workbook, the Modified Hepburn System is used, for the most part, to Romanize Japanese words and sentences. This widely used system comes the closest to representing the correct Japanese sounds and facilitates learning Japanese pronunciation. It is also known as the Hyōjun, or standard, System. (The original Hepburn System is no longer used, so references to the "Hepburn System" actually mean the Modified Hepburn System. The two are nearly identical, differing in only a few points.)

I would especially like to thank Barry Schilberg, who reviewed the manuscript and gave me invaluable suggestions from a student's point of view and patiently did the typing and detailed drafting work. He also assisted in the construction of the Hidden Word Puzzle in chapter 4.

I would also like to express my gratitude to my dear friend Virginia Newton for her help in editing the final text.

1

HOW TO WRITE SYLLABLES

The Japanese writing system consists of three types of symbols: *Hiragana*, *Katakana* and *Kanji*. Hiragana and Katakana (both of which are referred to simply as *Kana* symbols) are phonetic symbols and represent pronunciation, whereas Kanji are Chinese characters which have been assimilated into the Japanese language and express ideas or concepts. Because the Kana symbols are phonetic and represent pronunciation, they are somewhat similar in usage to the letters of the English alphabet. But Hiragana syllables constitute a syllabary, rather than an alphabet, and the same phonetic symbol always represents the same sound or combination of sounds, and vice versa. (In English the thirty-eight simplest sounds are represented by only twenty-six letters of the alphabet, so there is far less than one-to-one correspondence between symbol and sound. E.g. I, eye, by, buy, tie, etc.)

Hiragana and Katakana have their own unique functions. Hiragana underlies the basic structure of the writing system, whereas Katakana is limited in its usage to words of foreign origin, names of animals and plants and the like.

Hiragana is curvilinear in style and is considered by some to be harder to write than Katakana. For this reason, young children are sometimes taught Katakana before Hiragana. However, Hiragana, being more basic, should be learned first. Katakana can be introduced later.

One of the characteristics of Kana is that the symbols are syllabic symbols, which means that one Kana represents one syllable. There are five types of syllables in the Japanese language:

1. Five basic vowels: [a], [i], [u], [e], [o]

9

2. Consonant or semivowel + vowel: [na], [ki], [yu], etc.

3. Syllabic consonant: [n]/[m]

4. Any consonant other than [n]/[m] when followed by another identical consonant: e.g. *zasshi*, *gakkoo*, etc.

5. A contracted syllable: [ki] + [ya] = [kya], [chi] + [ya] = [cha], etc.

In the following sections of this chapter, the Hiragana symbols will be introduced, each one representing a syllable of one of these five types.

But before introducing the Hiragana, it is essential to point out the general rules for writing them.

First, it is important to memorize the correct stroke order (the sequence for writing the individual strokes of each symbol). The general rule for stroke order is left to right ⟶ and top to bottom ↓ .

Second, there are three different ways to end a stroke. These are called *tome*, *hane* and *harai*. Tome means "stop," so you must bring the pen or pencil to a complete stop and lift it off the paper at the end of the stroke. The tome ending is indicated by a period placed close to the last stroke in the following examples:

は. な.	や ま.	い え.
(flower)	(mountain)	(house)

The second ending, hane, means "jump." Therefore, you end the stroke with a reflex tail. This ending is indicated by a check mark √ in the following examples:

は た	か き	け さ
(flag)	(persimmon)	(this morning)

The third ending, harai, means "sweeping." You write this ending by lifting the pen or pencil up gradually at the end of the stroke while your hand is still in motion. This ending is indicated by a dotted line in the following examples:

(home)   (road)   (osushi)

You will note that some strokes do not have ending indicators. In these cases either the tome or the hane ending may be used.

On the following page is the complete Hiragana Syllabary. The first section of the table contains the forty-six basic symbols. The second and third sections contain the three forms of modification: *dakuon*, *handakuon* and *yōon*. Dakuon are syllables with voiced consonants, handakuon are syllables with semivoiced consonants, and yōon are contracted syllables.

After familiarizing yourself with the syllabary, turn to page 13 where you can begin learning Hiragana one group at a time, studying the text and doing the appropriate exercises. Each successive group of exercises includes Hiragana symbols from previous exercises.

TABLE I: HIRAGANA SYLLABARY

1. 46 Basic Hiragana

	n/m	wa	ra	ya	ma	ha	na	ta	sa	ka	a
a	ん	わ	ら	や	ま	は	な	た	さ	か	あ
i			り *ri*		み *mi*	ひ *hi*	に *ni*	ち *chi*	し *shi*	き *ki*	い *i*
u			る *ru*	ゆ *yu*	む *mu*	ふ *fu*	ぬ *nu*	つ *tsu*	す *su*	く *ku*	う *u*
e			れ *re*		め *me*	へ *he*	ね *ne*	て *te*	せ *se*	け *ke*	え *e*
o		を *o*	ろ *ro*	よ *yo*	も *mo*	ほ *ho*	の *no*	と *to*	そ *so*	こ *ko*	お *o*

2. 20 Dakuon and 5 Handakuon

	pa	ba	da	za	ga
a	ぱ	ば	だ	ざ	が
i	ぴ *pi*	び *bi*	ぢ *ji*	じ *ji*	ぎ *gi*
u	ぷ *pu*	ぶ *bu*	づ *zu*	ず *zu*	ぐ *gu*
e	ぺ *pe*	べ *be*	で *de*	ぜ *ze*	げ *ge*
o	ぽ *po*	ぼ *bo*	ど *do*	ぞ *zo*	ご *go*

3. 36 Yōon

21 Basic Yōon

rya	mya	hya	nya	cha	sha	kya
りゃ	みゃ	ひゃ	にゃ	ちゃ	しゃ	きゃ
りゅ *ryu*	みゅ *myu*	ひゅ *hyu*	にゅ *nyu*	ちゅ *chu*	しゅ *shu*	きゅ *kyu*
りょ *ryo*	みょ *myo*	ひょ *hyo*	にょ *nyo*	ちょ *cho*	しょ *sho*	きょ *kyo*

12 Voiced/3 Semivoiced

pya	bya	ja	ja	gya
ぴゃ	びゃ	ぢゃ	じゃ	ぎゃ
ぴゅ *pyu*	びゅ *byu*	ぢゅ *ju*	じゅ *ju*	ぎゅ *gyu*
ぴょ *pyo*	びょ *byo*	ぢょ *jo*	じょ *jo*	ぎょ *gyo*

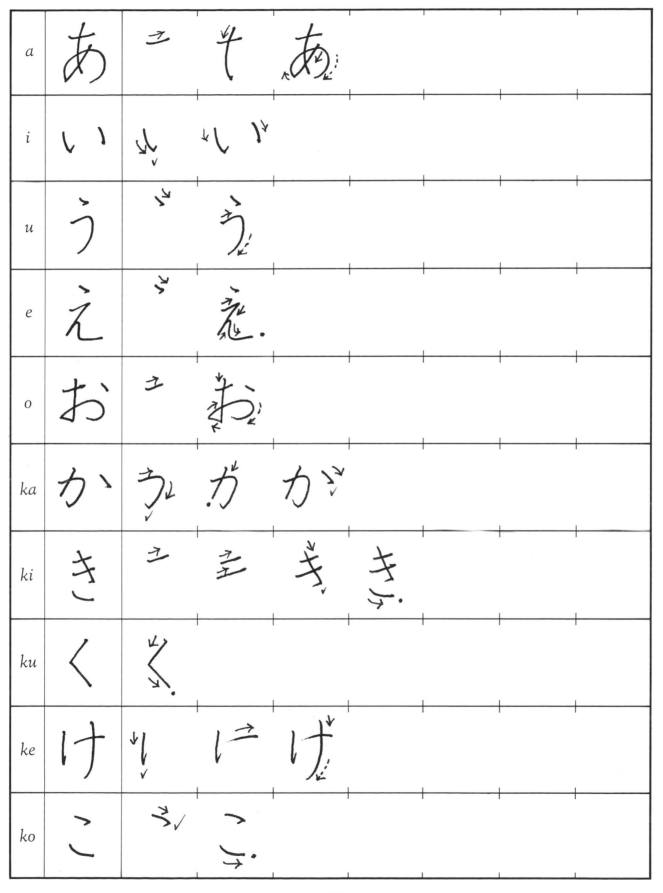

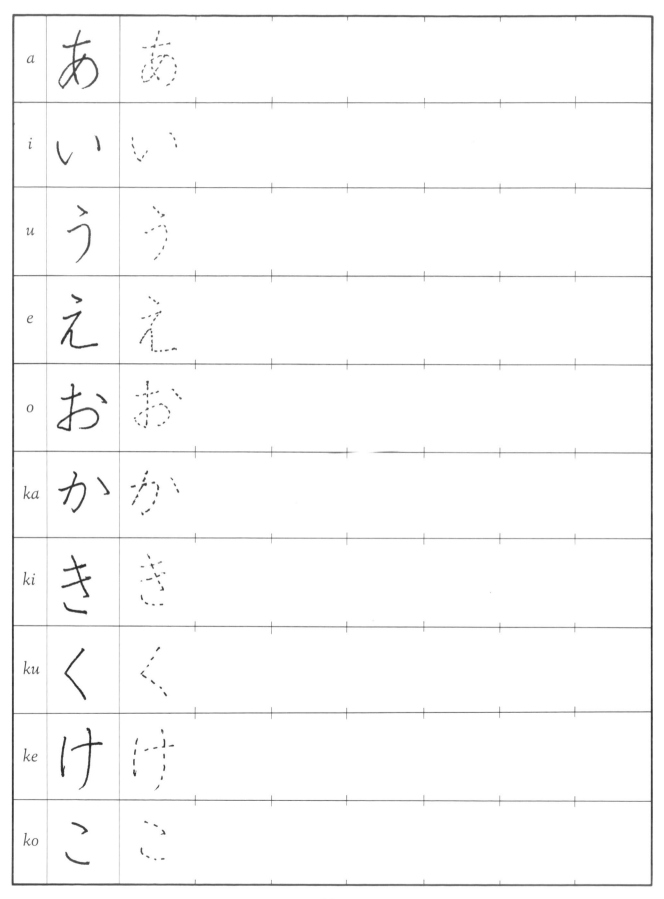

a	あ	あ
i	い	い
u	う	う
e	え	え
o	お	お
ka	か	か
ki	き	き
ku	く	く
ke	け	け
ko	こ	こ

First Group

As shown on the previous two pages, the first group of ten Hiragana consists of the five basic vowels, [a], [i], [u], [e], [o], and five syllables combining *k* with these vowels: [ka], [ki], [ku], [ke], [ko]. Practice writing the symbols over and over again until you have learned them, and then do the following exercises.

Exercises

A. Fill in each space with the appropriate Hiragana to make words.

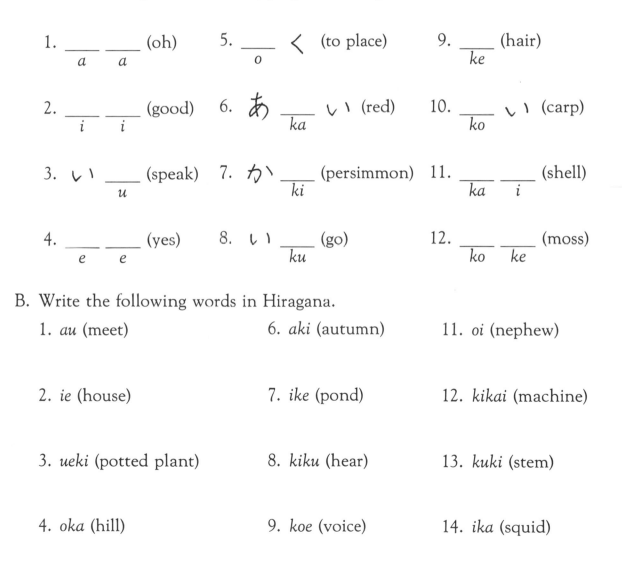

1. ___ ___ (oh)
     a *a*

2. ___ ___ (good)
     i *i*

3. い ___ (speak)
       u

4. ___ ___ (yes)
     e *e*

5. ___ く (to place)
    o

6. あ ___ い (red)
      ka

7. か ___ (persimmon)
      ki

8. い ___ (go)
      ku

9. ___ (hair)
   ke

10. ___ い (carp)
     ko

11. ___ ___ (shell)
     ka *i*

12. ___ ___ (moss)
     ko *ke*

B. Write the following words in Hiragana.

1. *au* (meet)
2. *ie* (house)
3. *ueki* (potted plant)
4. *oka* (hill)
5.
6. *aki* (autumn)
7. *ike* (pond)
8. *kiku* (hear)
9. *koe* (voice)
10.
11. *oi* (nephew)
12. *kikai* (machine)
13. *kuki* (stem)
14. *ika* (squid)

5. *kau* (buy)   10. *eki* (station)   15. *aku* (to be open)

C. Read the following words and write them in Romanized Japanese.

1. あかい (red)

2. あおい (blue)

3. いいえ (no)

4. うえ (top)

5. おおい (many)

6. かく (write)

7. かお (face)

8. けいこ (practice)

9. おおきい (big)

10. ここ (here)

11. あい (love)

12. えかき (artist)

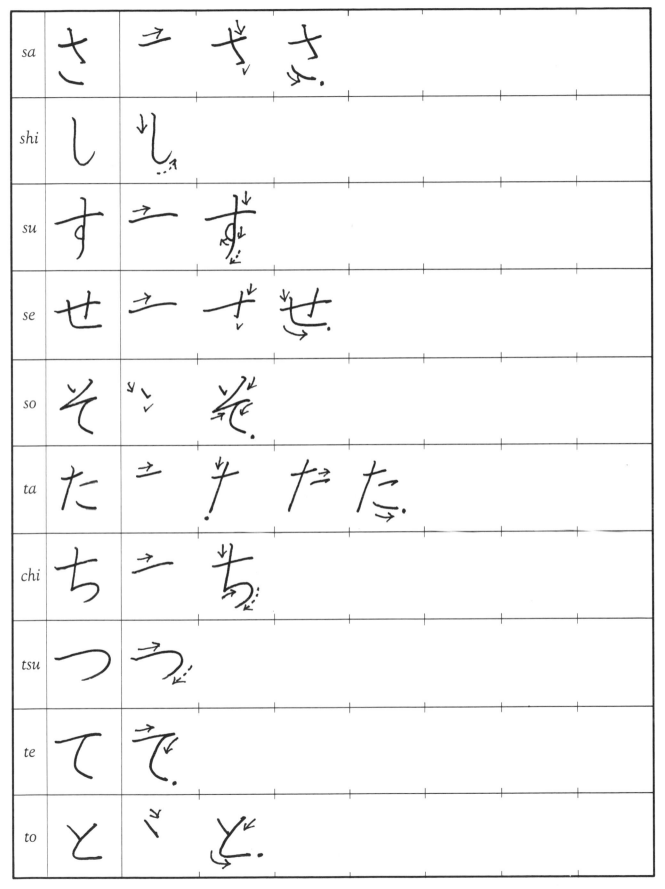

sa	さ			
shi	し			
su	す			
se	せ			
so	そ			
ta	た			
chi	ち			
tsu	つ			
te	て			
to	と			

sa	さ	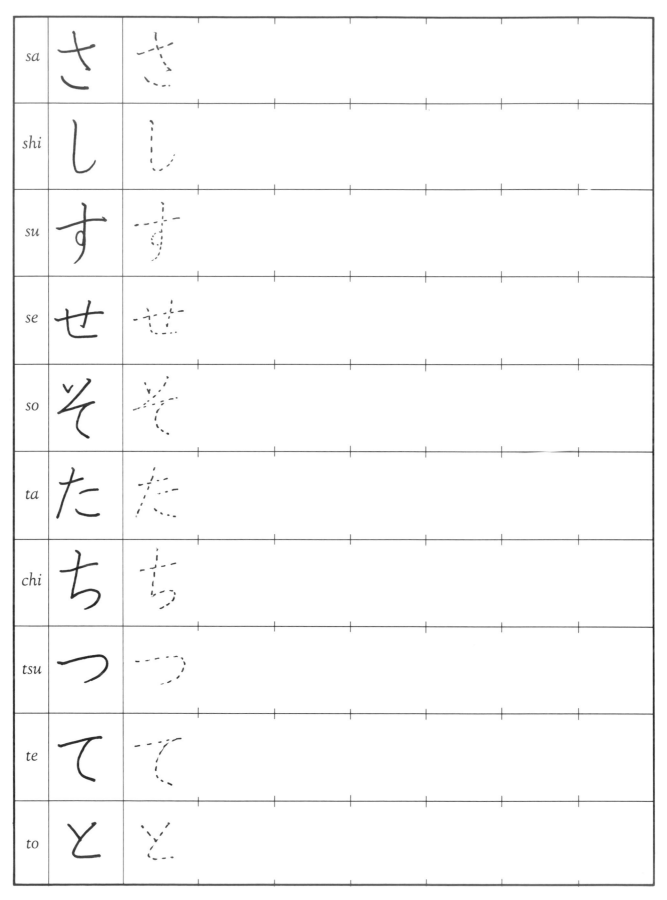
shi	し	
su	す	
se	せ	
so	そ	
ta	た	
chi	ち	
tsu	つ	
te	て	
to	と	

Second Group

The second group of ten Hiragana combines *s* or *t* with the basic vowels to form the syllables: [sa], [si], [su], [se], [so], [ta], [ti], [tu], [te], [to]. In the case of [si], [ti] and [tu], the pronunciations are closer to [shi], [chi] and [tsu], respectively, and they are thus represented in the Modified Hepburn System referred to in the preface and given in its entirety in table I on page 12. Therefore, [shi], [chi] and [tsu] are used throughout this book rather than [si], [ti] and [tu].

Exercises

D. Fill in the blanks with the appropriate Hiragana to make words.

1. あ ___ (morning)   5. ___ こ (there)   9. ___ (hand)
      sa   *so*   *te*

2. あ ___ (leg)   6. う ___ (song)   10. ___ (door)
      shi   *ta*   *to*

3. い ___ (chair)   7. ___ ___ (father) 11. く ___ (grass)
      su   *chi* *chi*   *sa*

4. ___ き (seat)   8. ___ き (moon)   12. い ___ (thread)
      se   *tsu*   *to*

E. Write the following words in Hiragana.

1. *kesa* (this morning)   5. *soto* (outside)   9. *tsukue* (desk)

2. *keshiki* (scenery)   6. *chikai* (near)   10. *sukoshi* (a little)

3. *seito* (student)   7. *suki* (liking)   11. *chiisai* (small)

4. *ashita* (tomorrow)   8. *katei* (home)   12. *ototoi* (day before yesterday)

19

F. Read the following words and write them in Romanized Japanese.

1. おすし (osushi)

2. おかし (sweets)

3. うち (house)

4. くつ (shoe)

5. あそこ (over there)

6. せかい (world)

7. おさけ (osake)

8. とけい (clock)

9. たかい (high)

10. ちかてつ (subway)

11. かさ (umbrella)

12. あつい (hot)

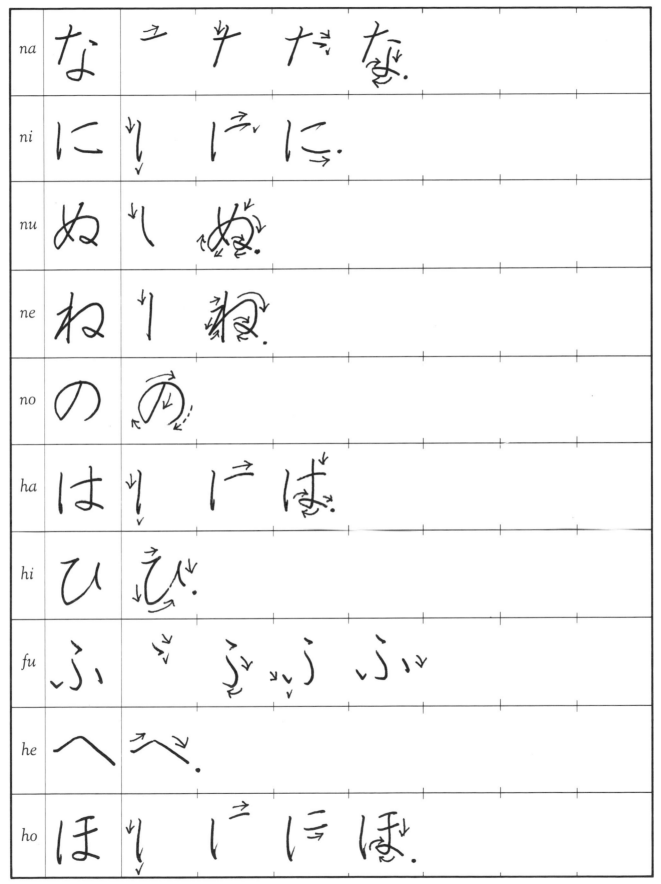

na	な	ニ	ナ	だ	な.
ni	に	り	に	に.	
nu	ぬ	し	ぬ.		
ne	ね	り	ね.		
no	の	の			
ha	は	り	に	ば.	
hi	ひ	び.			
fu	ふ	ふ	ふ	ふ	
he	へ	へ.			
ho	ほ	り	に	ほ.	

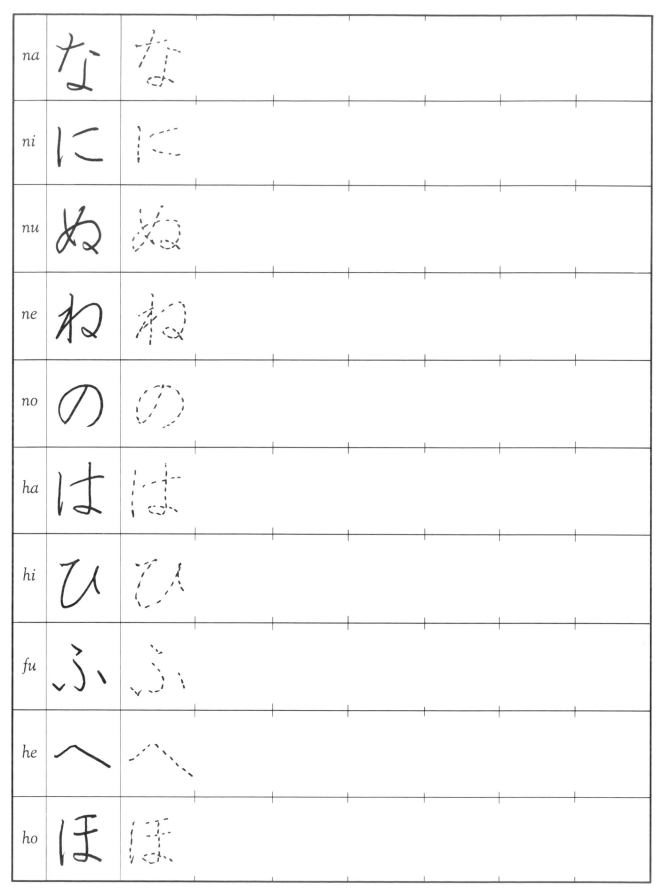

na	な	な
ni	に	に
nu	ぬ	ぬ
ne	ね	ね
no	の	の
ha	は	は
hi	ひ	ひ
fu	ふ	ふ
he	へ	へ
ho	ほ	ほ

Third Group

In the third group of ten Hiragana, *n* and *h* are combined with the basic vowels to form syllables, but there is one exception to this rule. These ten Hiragana are romanized as follows: [na], [ni], [nu], [ne], [no], and [ha], [hi], [fu], [he], [ho]. As you can see, the exception is the syllable [fu]. This change from *h* to *f* is necessary because the correct pronunciation (lips unrounded) produces a sound closer to the English [f] than to [h]. You should learn this exception well to avoid errors in pronunciation.

Exercises

G. Fill in the blanks with the appropriate Hiragana to make words.

1. か ___ (Kana)
      na

2. ___ く (meat)
   ni

3. き ___ (silk)
      nu

4. ___ こ (cat)
   ne

5. あ ___ (that over there)
      no

6. ___ こ (box)
   ha

7. ___ と (people)
   hi

8. ___ ___ (boat)
   fu *ne*

9. ___ た (unskillful)
   he

10. ___ し (star)
    ho

11. ___ ___ (flute)
    fu *e*

12. ___ ___ (flower)
    ha *na*

H. Write the following words in Hiragana.

1. *nani* (what)
2. *naka* (inside)
3. *kuni* (country)
4. *ani* (older brother)

7. *hane* (wing)
8. *ane* (older sister)
9. *sono* (that)
10. *hanashi* (story)

13. *hisui* (jade)
14. *fukai* (deep)
15. *futsuka* (2 days)
16. *heiki* (don't care)

5. *nishi* (west)　　11. *hatsuka* (20th day)　　17. *hoka* (other)

6. *nuu* (sew)　　12. *hikui* (low)　　18. *hone* (bone)

I. Read the following words and phrases and write them in Romanized Japanese.

1. あなた (you)　　8. ほし (star)

2. いぬ (dog)　　9. あかいはな (red flower)

3. おはし (chopsticks)　　10. ほそいあし (slender leg)

4. ふたつ (2)　　11. ちいさいふね (small boat)

5. にかい (2nd floor)　　12. へたなえ (poorly painted picture)

6. おかね (money)　　13. はこのなか (in a box)

7. ひとつ (1)　　14. すきなひと (a person one likes)

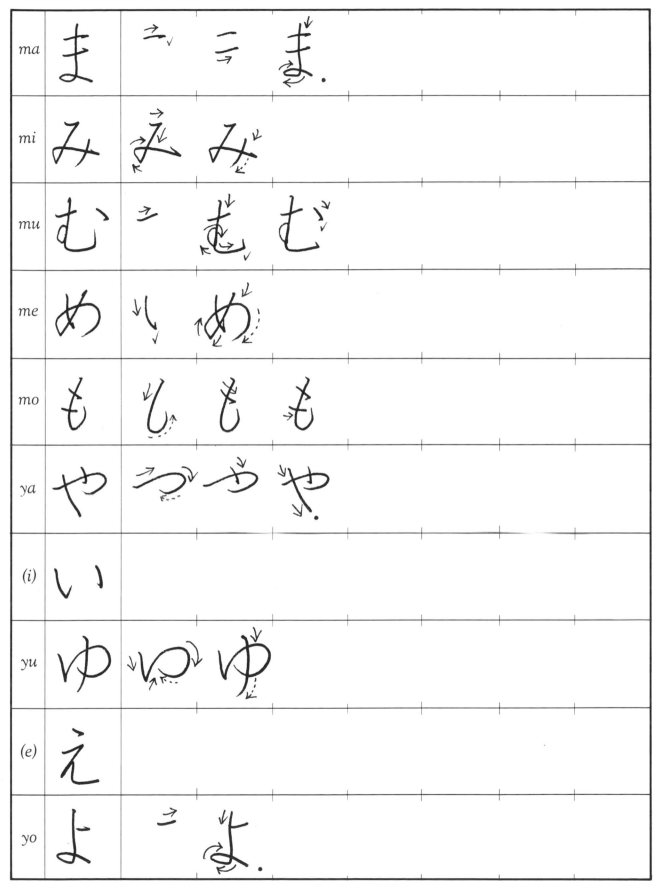

ma	ま			
mi	み			
mu	む			
me	め			
mo	も			
ya	や			
(i)	い			
yu	ゆ			
(e)	え			
yo	よ			

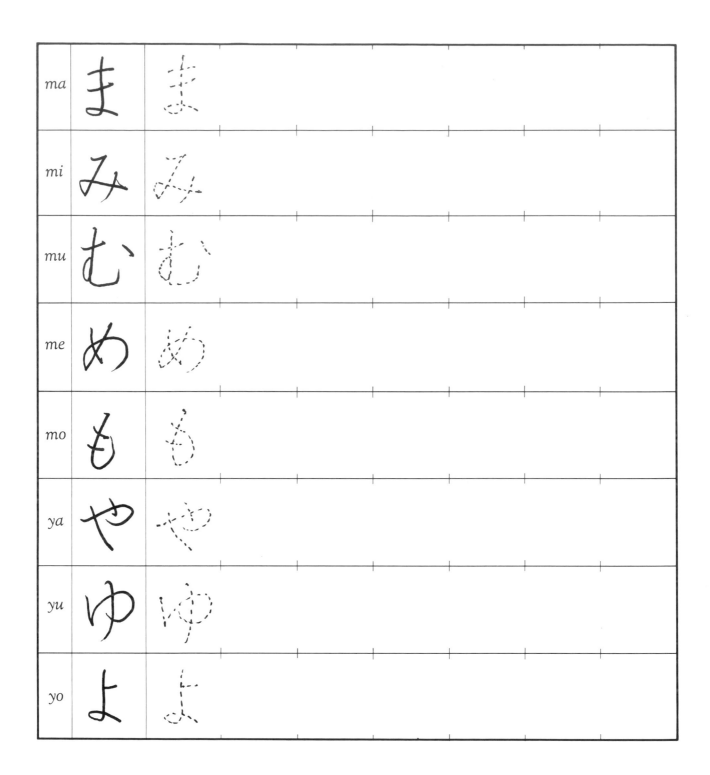

ma	ま	
mi	み	
mu	む	
me	め	
mo	も	
ya	や	
yu	ゆ	
yo	よ	

Fourth Group

In the fourth group of eight Hiragana, *m* and *y* are combined with basic vowels to form syllables. These are Romanized [ma], [mi], [mu], [me], [mo], and [ya], [yu], [yo]. You will note that there are only three symbols in the *y* subgroup. The other syllables, [yi] and [ye], do not exist in modern Japanese and can be considered duplicates of [i] and [e], respectively.

Exercises

J. Fill in the blanks with the appropriate Hiragana to make words.

1. ___ ち (town)
   ma

7. お ___ (hot water)
   yu

13. く ___ (cloud)
    mo

2. ___ ___ (ear)
   mi mi

8. ___ む (read)
   yo

14. ___ ね (roof)
    ya

3. の ___ (drink)
   mu

9. い ___ (now)
   ma

15. ___ か゛ (floor)
    yu

4. こ ___ (rice)
   me

10. う ___ (sea)
    mi

16. ___ い (good)
    yo

5. ___ ___ (peach)
   mo mo

11. す ___ (reside)
    mu

17. お ___ つ (snack)
    ya

6. へ ___ (room)
   ya

12. う ___ (plum)
    me

18. ___ え (front)
    ma

K. Write the following words in Hiragana:

1. *semai* (narrow)

9. *tsutsumu* (wrap)

17. *yasumi* (holiday)

2. *atama* (head)

10. *mukashi* (long ago)

18. *yasashii* (easy)

27

3. *shima* (island) 11. *tsumetai* (cold) 19. *oya* (parent)

4. *amai* (sweet) 12. *mei* (neice) 20. *yume* (dream)

5. *imi* (meaning) 13. *itsumo* (always) 21. *yukai* (pleasure)

6. *michi* (road) 14. *kimochi* (feeling) 22. *yuuhi* (setting sun)

7. *mise* (store) 15. *motsu* (hold) 23. *yoko* (side)

8. *nemui* (sleepy) 16. *hayai* (fast) 24. *kayou* (commute)

L. Read the following words and write them in Romanized Japanese.

1. まいにち (every day) 13. やすい (cheap)

2. なまえ (name) 14. すきやき (sukiyaki)

3. ひま (spare time) 15. ふゆ (winter)

4. かみ (paper) 16. ゆき (snow)

5. たたみ (tatami) 17. つよい (strong)

6. みな (all) 18. こよみ (calendar)

7. さむい (cold)

8. むすめ (daughter)

9. あめ (rain)

10. きもの (kimono)

11. かいもの (shopping)

12. やま (mountain)

19. うま (horse)

20. はさみ (scissors)

21. やさい (vegetables)

22. むし (insect)

23. にもつ (baggage)

24. せきゆ (petroleum)

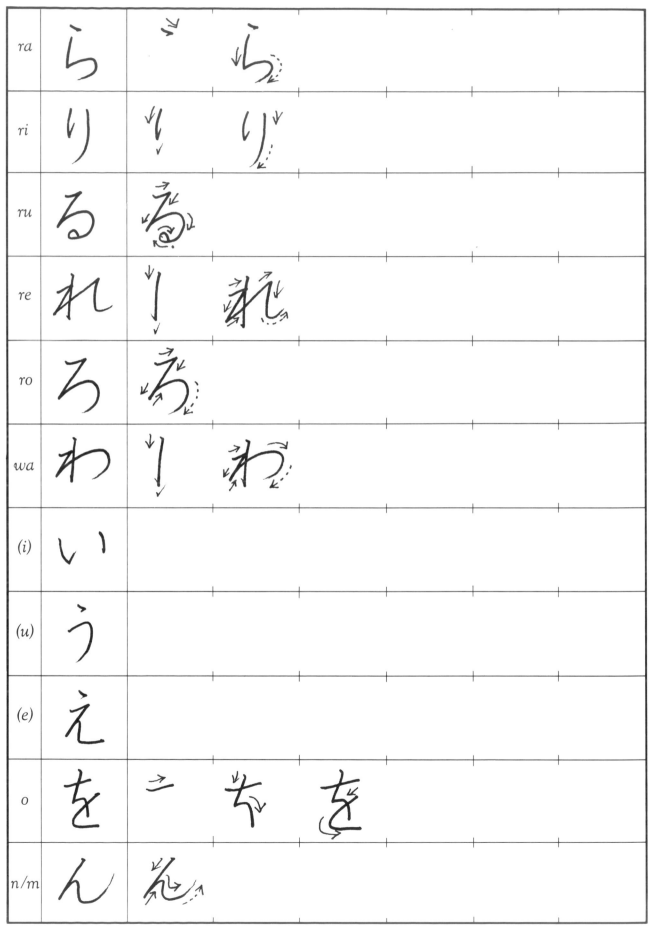

ra	ら	
ri	り	
ru	る	
re	れ	
ro	ろ	
wa	わ	
(i)	い	
(u)	う	
(e)	え	
o	を	
n/m	ん	

ra	ら	ら
ri	り	り
ru	る	る
re	れ	れ
ro	ろ	ろ
wa	わ	わ
o	を	を
n/m	ん	ん

Fifth Group

As shown on the preceding two pages, there are eleven symbols in the fifth group of Hiragana. However, as was the case with the fourth group, there are some duplicated syllables that were introduced earlier, so you only need to learn eight new symbols in this group. These are explained as follows.

The first five symbols combine *r* with the basic vowels to form syllables: [ra], [ri], [ru], [re], [ro]. The pronunciation of the Japanese [r] deserves careful attention because it produces a sound not found in English. It might be considered a cross between [r] and [l]. This sound is articulated by saying [r] while lightly touching the ridge behind the upper teeth once with the tip of the tongue, producing a flap [r]. This contrasts with curling the tip of the tongue back to produce the retroflex English [r].

The next, or sixth, symbol represents the syllable [wa], a combination of the semi-vowel [w] and the vowel [a]. The syllables [wi], [wu], [we] and [wo], which would be expected to complete this series, do not exist in modern Japanese. The first three can be considered duplicates of the vowels [i], [u] and [e]. The seventh symbol を is pronounced *o*, just like the vowel お [o]. This symbol を has a unique grammatical function, which will be explained later. Occasionally, you may come across the old symbols, ゐ and ゑ ; these are pronounced as [i] and [e], respectively. Because these symbols are not used in modern Japanese, you do not need to learn them.

The last (eighth) symbol in the fifth group represents the syllable [n]/[m]. The exact pronunciation of this symbol is dependent upon the phonetic context in which it occurs. The two pronunciations of the symbol ん are equivalent to either the English [n] or [m]. It is pronounced like [m] when it precedes [b], [m] or [p], and it is pronounced like [n] in all other cases. It is important to note that [n]/[m] is a syllable in itself and is different in this respect from the consonants [n] and [m] which, when followed by vowels, form other syllables, i.e., [na], [ni] . . . [ma], [mi] . . . and so on.

It is also important to know that the syllabic consonant [n]/[m] never begins a word, nor is it ever used consecutively.

Exercises

M. Fill in the blanks with the appropriate Hiragana to make words.

    1. そ ＿＿ (sky)　　　4. こ ＿＿ (this)　　　7. か ＿＿ (river)
          ra　　　　　　　　　　 *re*　　　　　　　　　　 *wa*

    2. も ＿＿ (forest)　　5. し ＿＿ (white)　　8. そ ＿＿ (that)
          ri　　　　　　　　　　 *ro*　　　　　　　　　　 *re*

    3. は ＿＿ (spring)　　6. ほ ＿＿ (book)　　9. と ＿＿ (bird)
          ru　　　　　　　　　　 *n*　　　　　　　　　　 *ri*

N. Write the following words in Hiragana:

    1. *tera* (temple)　　　6. *miru* (see)　　　11. *kaiwa* (conversation)

    2. *kirai* (disliking)　　7. *rekishi* (history)　　12. *wakai* (young)

    3. *tsuri* (fishing)　　　8. *kare* (that man)　　13. *minna* (all)

    4. *tonari* (neighbor)　　9. *hiroi* (wide)　　14. *ammari* (not very)

    5. *karui* (light in weight) 10. *ushiro* (back)　　15. *kantan* (simple)

O. Read the following words and write them in Romanized Japanese.

    1. さくら (cherry)　　　10. くろい (black)

    2. おさら (dish)　　　　11. きいろい (yellow)

    3. はり (needle)　　　　12. ところ (place)

4. あり (ant)

5. おわり (end)

6. ひる (noon)

7. よる (night)

8. あれ (that over there)

9. きれい (pretty)

13. わたくし (I)

14. かわいい (cute)

15. わるい (bad)

16. てんき (weather)

17. うんてん (driving)

18. おんなのひと (woman)

Dakuon

The three voiceless consonants, [k], [s] and [t] have voiced counterparts, and these are called *dakuon*. The voiced counterpart of [k] is [g], [s] is [z], and [t] is [d]. ([b] and [p] form a pair, too. *See* page 39.) The symbolic representation to indicate voicing of these consonants in Japanese is very systematic. Two abbreviated strokes are added at the upper right corner of each symbol. For example, you may recall that [ka] is represented by か , so [ga] is が , [ki] is き , [gi] is ぎ , and so on.

It is important to note that the voiced counterparts of し (*shi*) and ち (*chi*), which are じ (*ji*) and ぢ (*ji*), respectively, are pronounced the same. Likewise, the voiced counterparts of す (*su*) and つ (*tsu*), which are ず (*zu*) and づ (*zu*), are pronounced the same.

In answer to the question of when to use one or the other, we can say that in modern Japanese, じ (*ji*) and ず (*zu*) are most commonly used. However, ぢ (*ji*) and づ (*zu*) are still used occasionally, but only in the following cases.

1. In a compound word in which the original syllable was ち (*chi*), but the consonant became voiced as the result of compounding and a euphonic change, for example:

はな (nose) + ち (blood) → はなぢ (nosebleed)

こ (small) + つつみ (package) → こづつみ (postal package)

かん (can) + つめ (る) (cram) → かんづめ (canned food)

2. In a word in which ち (*chi*) and つ (*tsu*) repeat themselves, but the second ち (*chi*) and つ (*tsu*) are voiced due to a euphonic change, for example:

35

ち ぢ む (to shrink)

ちかぢか (near future) ← ち か (い) (near) + ち か (い) (near)

つ づ く (continue)

つきづき (monthly) ← つ き (month) + つ き (month)

Exercises

P. Fill in the blanks with the appropriate Hiragana to make words.

1. え い ___ (movie)
   _{ga}

13. な ___ (puzzle)
    _{zo}

2. か ___ (key)
   _{gi}

14. か ら ___ (body)
    _{da}

3. い そ ___ (hurry)
   _{gu}

15. ち ___ (map)
    _{zu}

4. ら い ___ つ (next month)
   _{ge}

16. う ___ (arm)
    _{de}

5. ___ ___ (afternoon)
   _{go} _{go}

17. ___ れ (which one)
    _{do}

6. か ___ り (decoration)
   _{za}

18. そ ___ (buckwheat noodles)
    _{ba}

7. さ ___ (spoon)
   _{ji}

19. え ___ (shrimp)
    _{bi}

8. あ ___ (taste)
   _{ji}

20. て ___ み (letter)
    _{ga}

9. か ___ (number)
   _{zu}

21. と ___ (jump)
    _{bu}

36

10. み ___ (water)
    zu

11. ___ ひ (by all means)
    ze

12. な ___ (why)
    ze

22. く ___ (nail)
    gi

23. か ___ (wall)
    be

24. ま ___ (window)
    do

Q. Write the following words in Hiragana.

1. *kagami* (mirror)

2. *kagaku* (science)

3. *hagaki* (post card)

4. *gin* (silver)

5. *uwagi* (coat)

6. *nugu* (undress)

7. *oyogu* (swim)

8. *kongetsu* (this month)

9. *Eigo* (English)

10. *shigoto* (work)

11. *fukuzatsu* (complicated)

12. *jikan* (time)

13. *jibun* (self)

14. *zuibun* (considerably)

15. *zeikin* (tax)

16. *daiji* (importance)

17. *denki* (electricity)

18. *tokidoki* (sometimes)

19. *kotoba* (word)

20. *bangohan* (dinner)

21. *hanabi* (fireworks)

22. *asobu* (play)

23. *benri* (convenient)

24. *obon* (tray)

R. Read the following words and write them in Romanized Japanese.

1. がくせい (student)

15. かぜ (wind)

2. いかが (how)

3. ながい (long)

4. めがね (glasses)

5. みぎ (right side)

6. にぎやか (lively)

7. すぐ (soon)

8. げんき (healthy)

9. にほんご (Japanese language)

10. ぎんざ (Ginza)

11. かんじ (Chinese characters)

12. なんじ (what time)

13. しずか (quiet)

14. ぜんぶ (whole)

16. かぞく (family)

17. だいがく (college)

18. でんわ (telephone)

19. どこ (where)

20. どなた (who)

21. こども (child)

22. かばん (briefcase)

23. こんばん (this evening)

24. ゆび (finger)

25. しんぶん (newspaper)

26. ふべん (inconvenient)

27. ぼんさい (dwarf tree)

28. ひだり (left)

Handakuon

Handakuon are the syllables beginning with *p*, which is the semivoiced counterpart of *b*. (*See* page 12.) This type of symbol is indicated by a little circle instead of two abbreviated strokes at the upper right hand corner of the syllables that begin with *h*, namely, ぱ, ぴ, ぷ, ぺ, ぽ.

As you may recall, the pronunciation of ふ is represented by [fu], because this denotes the correct pronunciation better than [hu] does. There is no corresponding change in the pronunciation of syllables that begin with *p*. These are pronounced like [pa], [pi], [pu], [pe], [po]. (Likewise, as seen in the previous section, there is no change in the syllables beginning with *b*.)

Exercises

S. Write the following words in Hiragana.

1. *parapara* (pitter patter)

2. *pikapika* (flashing)

3. *pekopeko* (cringe)

4. *paripari* (with a crunching sound)

5. *pachipachi* (crackling)

6. *pinpin* (lively)

7. *potopoto* (dripping)

8. *patapata* (flapping)

T. Read the following words and write them in Romanized Japanese.

1. しんぱい (worry)

2. かんぱい (toast)

3. えんぴつ (pencil)

5. おんぷ (musical notation)

6. きんぺん (vicinity)

7. ぽんぽん (with a bang)

4. てんぷら (tempura)　　　　8. さんぽ° (walk)

Yōon

The thirty-six contracted syllables consist of twenty-one basic yōon plus twelve where a consonant becomes voiced and three where a consonant becomes semivoiced.

All of the symbols that represent consonants combined with the vowel [i] (as shown in sections 1 and 2 of table I on page 12) make yōon (contracted syllables) when followed by [ya], [yu] or [yo]. Thus, [ki] + [ya] becomes [kya], [ki] + [yu] becomes [kyu] and [ki] + [yo] becomes [kyo]. The complete list of these contracted syllables can be seen in section 3 of table I. Note that the Hiragana representation of each of these syllables is made with a full-size Hiragana and a half-size [ya], [yu] or [yo]. All of the consonants form this combination in one of the three following ways.

1. $\dfrac{\text{C(onsonants)}}{\text{K,N,H,M,R}} + \text{Y} + \dfrac{\text{V(owels)}}{\text{A,U,O}}$

e.g. KI (き) + YO (よ)

K(I)YO (きょ), as in the *kyo* of *kyonen* (last year)

As indicated, in writing [ki] and [yo] together in *rōmaji* to form one syllable [kyo], you always delete the letter *i* in the first syllable: K(I) YO → KYO. Note that this KYO contrasts with the word KIYO (contribution). There are many similar cases.

2. $\dfrac{\text{C(onsonants)}}{\text{S or C}} + \text{H} + \dfrac{\text{V(owels)}}{\text{A,U,O}}$

e.g. CHI (ち) + YA (や)

CH(I)(Y)A (ちゃ), as in the *cha* of *ocha* (tea)

40

As indicated, pronouncing [chi] and [ya] together to form one syllable [cha] results in the deletion of the vowel [i] in the first syllable and the [y] in the second syllable. The same deletions are made when writing rōmaji.

3. $\dfrac{C(onsonant)}{J} + \dfrac{V(owels)}{A,U,O}$

    e.g. JI (じ) + YU (ゆ)

            J(I)(Y)U (じゅ), as in the *ju* of *shinju* (pearl)

As indicated, in combining [ji] and [yu] to produce the syllable [ju], the vowel [i] and the [y] are deleted.

Exercises

U. Fill in the spaces with the proper contracted sounds to make words.

1. ____ くせん   (passenger boat)
   kya

2. ____ うか   (vacation)
   kyu

3. ____ り   (distance)
   kyo

4. でん ____   (streetcar)
   sha

5. あく ____   (handshake)
   shu

6. さい ____   (the first)
   sho

7. ____ わん   (rice bowl)
   cha

8. ____ うい   (caution)
   chu

9. ____ しゃ   (author)
   cho

10. ____ うがく   (matriculation)
    nyu

11. ____ く   (100)
    hya

12. ____ く   (pulse)
    mya

13. ____ くじ   (abbreviated character)
    rya

14. ____ う   (dragon)
    ryu

15. ____ く ____   (green tea)
    ryo   *cha*

16. ____ しん   (photograph)
    sha

V. Write the following words in Hiragana, paying special attention to the underlined contracted syllables.

1. *kyakuma* (guest room)

2. *kyuushoku* (job hunting)

3. *senkyo* (election)

4. *oisha* (physician)

5. *renshuu* (practice)

6. *shujin* (husband)

7. *shokuji* (meal)

8. *akachan* (baby)

9. *chuusha* (injection)

10. *chokusetsu* (direct)

11. *nyuuin* (hospitalization)

12. *sammyaku* (mountain range)

13. *kiryuu* (air current)

14. *miryoku* (charm)

W. Read the following words and write them in Romanized Japanese.

1. おきゃく (guest)

2. けんきゅう (research)

3. きょねん (last year)

4. でんしゃ (train)

5. かいしゃ (company)

11. ちゅうがく (junior high school)

12. ちょきん (savings)

13. にゃあにゃあ (meow, meow)

14. ゆにゅう (import)

15. きゅうひゃく (900)

6. しゅくだい (homework)   16. ひゅうひゅう (with a whistle)

7. らいしゅう (next week)   17. ひょろひょろ (staggeringly)

8. としょかん (library)   18. りゃくれき (brief personal history)

9. ちゃいろ (brown)   19. りゅうがくせい (foreign student)

10. おちゃ (tea)   20. りょかん (inn)

X. Fill in each space with the proper contracted syllable to form a word.

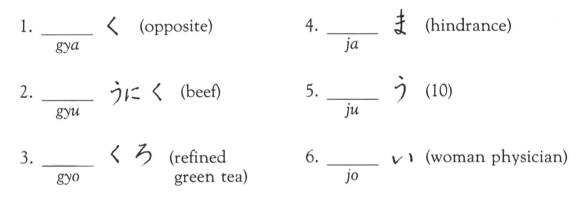

1. _____ く (opposite)
   gya

4. _____ ま (hindrance)
   ja

2. _____ うにく (beef)
   gyu

5. _____ う (10)
   ju

3. _____ くろ (refined green tea)
   gyo

6. _____ い (woman physician)
   jo

Y. Write the following words in Hiragana, paying special attention to the underlined contracted syllables.

1. *gyakuryuu* (backward current)

2. *jinja* (shrine)

3. *nijuu* (20)

4. *josei* (female)

6. *ningyo* (mermaid)

7. *juusho* (address)

8. *shinju* (pearl)

9. *bijutsukan* (art musuem)

5. *kinjo* (neighborhood)   10. *gyosen* (fishing boat)

Z. Read the following words and write them in Romanized Japanese.

1. ぎゃくせつ (paradox)   6. ぎゅうにゅう (milk)

2. きんぎょ (goldfish)   7. かんじゃ (patient)

3. きゅうじゅう (90)   8. かのじょ (she)

4. さんびゃく (300)   9. びゅうびゅう (howlingly)

5. ぴゅうぴゅう (hisses)   10. ぴょんぴょん (hop)

2

HOW TO WRITE WORDS

Now that you have learned how to write all of the Hiragana symbols, the next step is to learn how to use them in writing words. In order to do this you must first identify the syllables and then write each one in Hiragana. In other words, you write one Hiragana for each syllable, for example:

a ka i (red)   *ka mi* (paper)   *tsu ku e* (desk)

あ か い   か み   つ く え

There are several important rules to be observed in writing words. Let us consider them one by one in the following sections of this chapter.

Syllabic Consonant [n]/[m]

As noted on page 32, this syllable, whether pronounced [n] or [m], is written with the symbol ん . If [n] or [m] is followed by another consonant, or if a word ends with [n] or [m], then that [n] or [m] is, without exception, a syllable in itself. However, if a vowel (*a, i, u, e, o*) follows *n* or *m*, then it will not be immediately apparent whether it is a syllable or simply one part of a syllable. For example, if not correctly written the word *ta n'i* (unit) might be mistaken for *ta ni* (valley). In such a case, you must know the word by rote in order to be able to write it correctly in Hiragana. Do the following exercises to become familiar with the syllabic consonant [n]/[m].

Exercises

A. Write the following words in Hiragana, paying special attention to the underlined syllabic consonant.

1. *o<u>n</u>gaku* (music)   5. *he<u>n</u>ji* (answer)   9. *ze<u>m</u>bu* (whole)

45

2. *mon* (gate)   6. *kin* (gold)   10. *kondo* (this time)

3. *shimpo* (progress)   7. *genkan* (entrance)   11. *fuben* (inconvenient)

4. *kantan* (simple)   8. *sampo* (walk)   12. *gin* (silver)

B. Write the following words in Hiragana.

1. *bungaku* (literature)   8. *ningen* (human being)

2. *nammai* (how many sheets)   9. *ammari* (not very)

3. *sentaku* (laundry)   10. *benri* (convenient)

4. *nannin* (how many people)   11. *sonnani* (not very)

5. *mannaka* (center)   12. *sensei* (teacher)

6. *ninki* (popularity)   13. *anshin* (relief)

7. *komban* (this evening)   14. *kankei* (relation)

C. Read the following words and write them in Romanized Japanese.

1. にほんご (Japanese)   9. おんな (woman)

2. てんき (weather)　　　　10. はんぶん (half)

3. しんぶん (newspaper)　　11. げんき (healthy)

4. みんな (all)　　　　　　12. かばん (briefcase)

5. うんてん (driving)　　　13. ほんばこ (bookcase)

6. りんご (apple)　　　　　14. かんじ (Chinese characters)

7. たいへん (very)　　　　15. せんしゅう (last week)

8. えんぴつ (pencil)　　　16. あんき (memorize)

Double Vowel [o]+[o]

Another point which deserves special attention concerns the writing of double o's (oo) (ō in the Hepburn System). When double o's occur, the second [o] syllable is written with an う [u] in most cases. The few exceptions to this rule should be memorized as they are encountered. (Some of the exceptions are given in the exercises that follow.)

Other double vowels should be written as they are pronounced, as illustrated in the following examples. (Romanization is not completely standardized; *ii* and *ee* are common but both *aa* and *ā* will be encountered. Double *u* is usually *ū*.)

o ka <u>a</u> sa n (mother)　　　o ni <u>i</u> sa n (older brother)
おかあさん　　　　　　　　おにいさん

47

fu u fu (husband and wife)   *o ne e sa n* (older sister)

ふうふ   おねえさん

You should also be aware that there are many word pairs which look alike except for a repeated vowel in one of them that makes a difference in the meaning. Here are a few examples:

o ba sa n (aunt)   ⟷   o ba a sa n (grandmother)

o ji sa n (uncle)   ⟷   o ji i sa n (grandfather)

i e (house)   ⟷   i i e (no)

yo ji (4 o'clock)   ⟷   yo o ji (business)

ni n gyo (mermaid)   ⟷   ni n gyo o (doll)

Exercises

D. Write the following words in Hiragana, using う for the second [o].

1. *doozo* (please)   4. *kinoo* (yesterday)   7. *booshi* (hat)

2. *kyoo* (today)   5. *kookoo* (high school)   8. *hontoo* (truth)

3. *ginkoo* (bank)   6. *yooka* (8th day)   9. *jidoosha* (automobile)

E. Write the following words in Hiragana, paying particular attention to the second [o].

1. *hikooki* (airplane)   6. *imooto* (younger sister)

2. *mukoo* (over there)   7. *sooji* (cleaning)

3. *yooi* (preparation)   8. *senkoo* (major)

4. *Tookyoo* (Tokyo)   9. *Toodai* (Tokyo University)

5. *kooen* (park)   10. *hoobi* (reward)

F. Read the following words and write them in Romanized Japanese.

1. おとうさん (father)   6. そうです (it is so)

2. おとうと (younger brother)   7. とうとう (finally)

3. さようなら (goodbye)   8. きょうと (Kyoto)

4. じょうず (skillful)   9. びょういん (hospital)

5. べんきょう (study)   10. りょこう (trip)

G. The second [o] in the following words is written with お (not with う)
Write these words in Hiragana.

1. *ooi* (many)   5. *Oosaka* (Osaka)   9. *tooru* (pass through)

2. *ookii* (big)   6. *oodoori* (main street)   10. *ookami* (wolf)

3. *too* (10)   7. *toori* (street)   11. *koori* (ice)

4. *tooi* (far)   8. *hoo* (cheek)   12. *oou* (to cover)

49

H. Compare the following pairs of words and then write them in Hiragana.

1. *o ba sa n* (aunt) ⟷ *o ba a sa n* (grandmother)

2. *o ji sa n* (uncle) ⟷ *o ji i sa n* (grandfather)

3. *ni n gyo* (mermaid) ⟷ *ni n gyo o* (doll)

4. *to ri* (bird) ⟷ *to o ri* (street, road)

5. *i e* (house) ⟷ *i i e* (no)

6. *yo ji* (4 o'clock) ⟷ *yo o ji* (business)

Double Consonants

Writing double consonants other than [n] and [m] in Kana is very systematic and there are no exceptions. Whenever double consonants occur, no matter which consonants they are, the first of the pair is always written with a half-size [tsu], i.e. っ . Observe the following examples:

| *Ni p̱ po n* (Japan) | *ga k̲ kō* (school) | *za s̲ shi* (magazine) |
| にっぽん | がっこう | ざっし |

The half-size [tsu] っ , as used here, almost always symbolizes a time beat of the same duration as one syllable.

The double consonant [n]/[m] is not to be treated as shown above, but rather as a syllable followed by a consonant that is the first part of the following syllable. The first consonant, [n] or [m], is written with the syllabic symbol ん as shown in the following examples:

mi <u>*n*</u> <u>*na*</u> (everybody)   *a* <u>*m*</u> <u>*ma*</u> *ri* (not very)   *so* <u>*n*</u> <u>*na*</u> *ni* (not so much)

みんな   あんまり   そんなに

Exercises

I. Write the following words in Hiragana, paying special attention to the first underlined consonant:

1. *ma* <u>*s*</u> *shi ro* (pure white)

2. *ki* <u>*p*</u> *pu* (ticket)

3. *mi* <u>*t*</u> *tsu* (3)

4. *ni* <u>*k*</u> *ki* (diary)

5. *sa* <u>*k*</u> *ki* (a few minutes ago)

6. *chi* <u>*t*</u> *to mo* (not at all)

7. *mi* <u>*k*</u> *ka* (3 days)

8. *i* <u>*k*</u> *ke n* (1 house)

J. First divide each word into syllables, then write it in Hiragana.

1. *yottsu* (4)

2. *atchi* (over there)

3. *ippai* (1 glassful)

4. *sekken* (soap)

5. *isshoni* (together)

6. *kitte* (stamp)

7. *kitto* (by all means)

8. *gakki* (musical instrument)

9. *motto* (more)

10. *rippa* (wonderful)

11. *kekkon* (marriage)

12. *hassen* (8,000)

K. Read the following words and write them in Romanized Japanese.

1. がっこう (school)

2. むっつ (6)

3. にっぽん (Japan)

4. いっぽん (1 slender object)

5. いっかい (1st floor)

6. はっさつ (8 volumes)

7. ろっぽん (6 slender objects)

8. じっぽん (10 slender objects)

9. はっぱい (8 cupfuls)

10. はっぴゃく (800)

11. よっか (4th day)

12. いっぷん (1 minute)

13. やっつ (8)

14. こっち (here)

15. ざっし (magazine)

16. いったい (what on earth)

17. いっさつ (1 volume)

18. じっさつ (10 volumes)

19. はっぽん (8 slender objects)

20. ろっぱい (6 cupfuls)

21. じっぱい (10 cupfuls)

22. ろっぴゃく (600)

23. あさって (day after tomorrow)

24. しっぱい (failure)

When Japanese is written vertically and a syllabic symbol is repeated consecutively in the same word, the symbol of repetition ゝ can be used, as shown in the following examples:

(tatami)   (plum)   (scarecrow)   (bamboo leaf)

Note that if the second symbol represents the voiced counterpart of the first symbol, then the convention for the voiced consonant ゛ applies to the symbol of repetition ゞ.

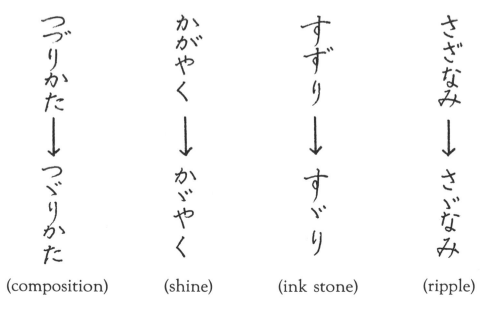

(composition)   (shine)   (ink stone)   (ripple)

There are some cases in which the symbols of repetition may not be used even though a word has the same syllables in consecutive order. These exceptions are as follows:

1. If the word is borrowed from another language. (Such words are written in Katakana.) For example, バナナ (banana), ココア (*kokoa*, cocoa)

2. If the syllabic repetition is a necessary part of the conjugation of a verb or an adjective. かかない (do/does not write), あわてて (helter-skelter), かわいい (cute), たかかった (was/were expensive)

3. If the word is a compound word. のみみず (*nomu* + *mizu*, drinking water), そののち (*sono* + *nochi*, after that), いままで (*ima* + *made*, until now)

Exercise

L. Rewrite the following words using the symbol of repetition ヽ or ゞ .

1.	2.	3.	4.	5.	6.
もも	みみ	ええ	かがみ	ただ	いかが
(peach)	(ear)	(yes)	(mirror)	(free)	(how)
7.	8.	9.	10.	11.	12.
ちち	いいえ	ああ	ななつ	おおきい	ここ
(father)	(no)	(oh)	(seven)	(large)	(here)

The repetition of two or more syllables can be indicated as follows. This symbol 〱 is used in vertical writing only, and always occupies two writing spaces.

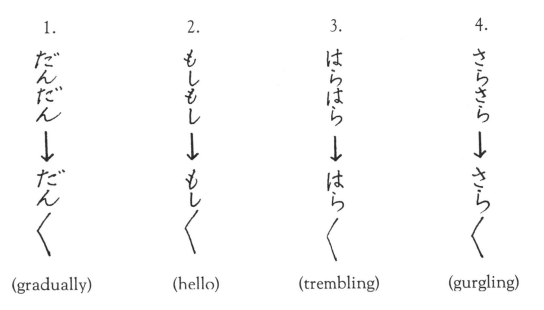

1.	2.	3.	4.
(gradually)	(hello)	(trembling)	(gurgling)

Note again that if the repeated part has a voiced consonant, you can use the convention for the voiced counterpart with the symbol of repetition. Observe the following examples:

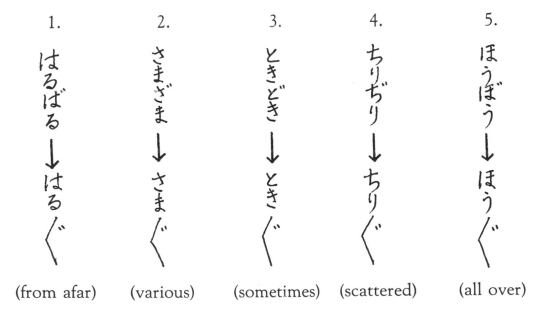

1.	2.	3.	4.	5.
(from afar)	(various)	(sometimes)	(scattered)	(all over)

Although these symbols of repetition, 〻 and 〳 , are no longer used officially, they are still acceptable for daily usage.

Exercise

M. Rewrite the following words using the symbol 〳 or 〴 :

1.	2.	3.	4.
ぶらぶら	たびたび	わざわざ	ちかぢか
(leisurely)	(often)	(making a special effort)	(near future)

5.	6.	7.	8.
つくづく	いきいき	とうとう	いろいろ
(thoroughly)	(vividly)	(finally)	(various)

3

HOW TO WRITE SENTENCES

Particles *wa*, *o* and *e*

Having learned how to write words in Hiragana, the next step is learning how to write sentences. This requires that you first learn some conventions for writing particles. The three particles that you must learn first are: *wa* (for the sentence topic), *e* (for direction), and *o* (for the direct object).

The particle *wa*, pronounced just like the syllable [wa], is always written with は rather than わ. The particle *e*, pronounced like [e], is represented by へ rather than え. The particle *o*, pronounced like [o], is written with を rather than お. Study the following examples.

1. *Konnichi wa.* (Hello.)

   こんにちは。

2. *Watashi wa seito desu.* (I am a student.)

   わたし は せいとです。

3. *Doko e ikimasu ka.* (Where are you going?)

   どこへ いきますか。

4. *Gakkō e ikimasu.* (I am going to school.)

   がっこうへ いきます。

5. *Gakkō de nani o shimasu ka.* (What are you going to do at school?)

   がっこうで なにをします か。

6. *Benkyō o shimasu.* (I am going to study.)

   べんきょうをします。

Exercise

A. Write the following sentences in Hiragana, paying special attention to *wa*, *e* and *o*.

1. *Kyō wa ii otenki desu ne. Gakkō wa dō desu ka.*

2. *Omoshiroi desu. Mainichi Nihongo no benkyō o shimasu.*

3. *Sore wa kekkō desu ne. Gogo nani o shimasu ka.*

4. *Toshokan e ikimasu. Soshite hon o yomimasu. Anata wa.*

5. *Watashi wa kaisha e ikimasu. Soshite shigoto o shimasu.*

Punctuation

In Japanese, the punctuation mark (*kutōten*) that is comparable to the English comma is 、 , and the Japanese equivalent of the English period is 。 . Quotation marks in Japanese are 「 」 for writing horizontally, and 「 」 for writing vertically. Note the following examples:

わたしはてんぷらをたべますが、たろうさんはおすしをたべます。

(I will eat tempura but Taroo will eat sushi.)

「たなかさん、おはようございます。いかがですか。」「おかげさまで
げんきです。あなたは。」

("Good morning, Mr. Tanaka. How are you?" "I am fine, thank you. And you?")

58

When these sentences are written vertically, the punctuation appears as follows:

わたしは てんぷらを たべますが、たろうさんは
おすしを たべます。

「たなかさん、おはよう ございます。
いかがですか。」

「おかげさまで げんきです。あなたは。」

As in English, the rules governing the use of the Japanese comma are not inflexible. It is generally used in those places where it is necessary to avoid a misunderstanding in the intended meaning of the sentence. There is no Japanese equivalent of the English question mark because the particle *ka* indicates a question.

4

REVIEW EXERCISES

On the following pages are several kinds of exercises designed to give practice in using the Hiragana you have now mastered.

Part A of the exercises shows some of the common mistakes that students make when they read and write Hiragana. It is best to review these common mistakes before doing the exercises in parts B, C, D and E.

The two exercises B and C deal with the recognition of Hiragana, and part D involves the correction of mistakes in writing. Part E emphasizes the writing of Hiragana. You should attempt to do these exercises as rapidly as possible without making mistakes.

A. Common Mistakes

1. Hiragana that look alike or are often confused with each other:

a. あ　　お　　　　　g. ね　　ぬ

b. い　　こ　　　　　h. は　　ほ

c. う　　ら　　　　　i. ま　　も

d. さ　　き　　　　　j. め　　ぬ

e. さ　　ち　　　　　k. る　　ろ

f. な　　た　　　　　l. わ　　れ

2. Hiragana that are often written incorrectly:

a. カ for か　　　　d. さ for ち

b. 〉 for く　　　　e. は for ほ

c. ⌡ for し　　　　f. ま for ま

61

B. Recognition Exercise

Find the Hiragana symbol that matches each Romanized syllable written to the left of the vertical line. Try to go as fast as you can, avoiding mistakes.

u	み	つ	ら	う	ち	さ	お
ka	わ	か	け	や	み	つ	ゆ
pyo	ひゃ	びゅ	ぴゃ	びょ	ぴょ	ぴゅ	びゃ
se	ゆ	せ	け	や	そ	さ	み
ho	も	は	ま	な	ほ	け	せ
wa	ゆ	れ	ね	ぬ	め	わ	あ
e	ち	り	い	う	さ	ら	え
chi	さ	ら	ち	き	う	す	を
n	な	ひ	け	そ	え	と	ん
ki	せ	さ	き	ま	ほ	も	け
re	わ	ね	ぬ	れ	ろ	け	ゆ
gya	じゃ	ぎゃ	ぎゅ	きゃ	きょ	びゃ	じゅ
o	あ	お	わ	め	ろ	る	の
yu	こ	に	み	ゆ	ね	よ	や
ma	き	ま	ほ	も	さ	な	よ
nu	あ	ゆ	ね	れ	ぬ	め	の
bu	ぶ	ぞ	べ	ざ	び	ば	ぼ
to	く	ろ	て	と	そ	を	ひ
a	お	あ	ぬ	ろ	め	わ	の
su	よ	む	を	ち	た	す	さ
jo	ぎょ	じゃ	びょ	ぢゃ	じょ	じゅ	ぢゅ
ge	げ	ぞ	ぜ	ご	ぼ	ば	だ
i	こ	く	し	り	い	に	て

C. Hidden Word Puzzle

At the bottom of the page there are forty words written in Roman letters. Try to find them in the Hiragana maze. The words may be written from left to right, top to bottom or diagonally (left to right only). No words are written backwards. Circle them as you find them. There may be other hidden words besides those listed. See how many you can find.

ら	え	じゅ	ん	か	ん	き	の	う	ま	こ	じゃ	そ	け	む	ふ	せ	え
に	な	つ	を	さ	げ	あ	お	ちゅ	の	づ	ぺ	き	い	ろ	い	ま	ん
れ	の	ぺ	う	ほ	ぎゃ	ふ	ちゃ	べ	く	つ	ぜ	を	う	の	ぴゃ	さ	ぎゅ
ん	こ	じょ	ゆ	ね	の	ぢゅ	ぜ	や	い	み	ほ	け	ら	ぬ	ぢ	お	う
しゅ	お	あ	り	が	と	う	わ	ふ	れ	ま	が	そ	ご	ひ	ふ	よ	に
う	し	た	か	ぼ	や	る	ず	ぐ	ゆ	げ	く	ゆ	ぜ	る	びゅ	ぐ	く
ま	に	が	あ	み	さ	ふ	く	ざ	つ	ぬ	せ	う	ぼ	を	み	ね	だ
だ	ぞ	ん	り	う	い	つ	ほ	しょ	ん	びゃ	い	ぐ	ぴょ	う	ちょ	の	で
を	ぷ	ご	ぎょ	じ	に	び	ご	か	ど	ひゃ	も	じゃ	こ	え	し	ご	と
きょ	う	る	さ	う	な	か	りょ	じ	べ	ぱ	く	ま	は	む	か	ざ	る
の	りゃ	な	よ	れ	にゅ	ね	さ	じょ	を	づ	れ	へ	あ	お	い	は	ら
じょ	く	ゆ	う	ぎょ	き	び	か	て	の	ん	あ	に	ほ	ん	ご	わ	ぼ
む	じ	ぼ	な	あ	だ	さ	な	む	さ	る	ぞ	しゃ	と	あ	べ	こ	う
ひゃ	う	こ	ら	が	っ	こ	う	あ	ね	ぼ	ち	て	ぜ	し	う	か	わ
ゆ	く	ね	ぼ	う	ざ	を	か	へ	げ	きゃ	ぷ	ご	が	た	け	し	も
の	ぢ	れ	で	の	ほ	お	ぞ	りゅ	う	が	く	せ	い	み	そ	う	ろ

natsu	ojōsan	fuyu	gakusei	hyaku	kozutsumi	oyogu	kyō
ushiro	ashita	aoi	jama	haru	gakkō	yasai	renshū
umi	zehi	nebō	gyūniku	ocha	kinō	okāsan	ryokan
tegami	kyaku	ningyō	myōji	ryūgakusei	ryakuji	shigoto	sayōnara
naka	arigatō	sakana	Nihongo	aki	kiiroi	mae	fukuzatsu

63

D. Correction Exercise

In the following list of words there are some that are written incorrectly in Hiragana. Find the mistakes and write the words correctly.

Example: Nihongo に はんご
　　　　　　　　ほ

1. yasashii やさし
2. senkyo せえんきょ
3. benri べんり
4. jūsho じうしょ
5. bungaku ぶんがく
6. obāsan おばさん
7. Nippon にぼん
8. masshiro まっしろ
9. chawan ちあわん
10. hikōki ひこおき

16. mannaka まなか
17. anshin あんしん
18. kenkyū けんきゅ
19. Tōkyō とおきょう
20. ryakuji りゃくじ
21. pachipachi ばちばち
22. fukuzatsu ふくずつ
23. sammyaku さんみゃく
24. chokusetsu ちょくせっ
25. ōdōri おおとおり

64

11. kyakuma　きゃくま　　26. chittomo　ちとも

12. shimpo　しんぼ゙　　27. keshiki　けしき

13. bijutsukan　びじうっすかん　28. nyūin　にゅうにん

14. sonnani　そっなに　　29. toshokan　としょうかん

15. josei　じょうせぃ　　30. ningyō　にんぎょ

E. Writing Exercise

Write the following dialogues in Hiragana in the space provided below each line. Punctuate the sentences using the Japanese *kutōten* introduced in this book.

1. Y: "Tanaka-san, konnichi wa."
   (Good day, Mr. Tanaka.)

   T: "Ah, Yamada-san, shibaraku desu ne. Ogenki desu ka."
   (Oh, Mr. Yamada, it's been a while, hasn't it? How are you?)

   Y: "Ee, okagesamade genki desu. Anata wa."
   (I'm fine, thank you. And you?)

   T: "Arigatō gozaimasu. Watashi mo aikawarazu desu."
   (I'm fine as usual, thank you.)

Y: "Sore wa kekkō desu ne."
(That's fine, isn't it.)

2. T: "Kyō wa ii otenki desu ne. Gakkō wa dō desu ka."
(Today the weather is good, isn't it. How is school?)

Y: "Totemo omoshiroi desu."
(It's very interesting.)

T: "Sō desu ka. Nani ga ichiban omoshiroi desu ka."
(Is that right? What's most interesting to you?)

Y: "Shinrigaku ga ichiban omoshiroi desu."
(Psychology is most interesting.)

T: "Anata no senkō wa nan desu ka."
(What is your major?)

Y: "Watashi no senkō wa shakaigaku desu. Anata wa nan no benkyō o
(My major is sociology. What are you studying?)

shite imasu ka."

T: "Watashi no senkō wa mada kimatte imasen ga, shōrai kaikeigaku no
(My major is undecided, as yet. But in the future I'm thinking of study-

benkyō o shitai to omotte imasu."
ing accounting.)

3. Y: "Tanaka-san, ohayō gozaimasu. Kinō wa nani o shimashita ka."
(Good morning, Mr. Tanaka. What did you do yesterday?)

T: "Kaimono ni ikimashita. Soshite Nihongo no jibiki o issatsu kaima-
(I went shopping. Then I bought a Japanese dictionary. And you?)

shita. Anata wa."

Y: "Watashi wa kaisha e ikimashita. Soshite shigoto o shimashita."
(I went to my company. Then I did some work.)

T: "Anata no kaisha wa jidōsha no kaisha desu ne. Uchi kara tōi desu
(Your company is an automobile company, isn't it? Is it far from your

ka."
house?)

67

Y: "Iie, sonnani tōku nai desu. Kuruma de jūgo fun gurai desu."
(No, not so far. It takes about fifteen minutes by car.)

T: "Sore wa benri desu ne."
(That's convenient, isn't it?)

APPENDIX A: Quiz Answers

Correction Exercise (p. 64)

1. やさしい	11. Correct	21. ぱちぱち
2. せんきょ	12. しんぽ	22. ふくざつ
3. Correct	13. びじゅつかん	23. さんみゃく
4. じゅうしょ	14. そんなに	24. Correct
5. Correct	15. じょせい	25. おおどおり
6. おばあさん	16. まんなか	26. ちっとも
7. にっぽん	17. Correct	27. Correct
8. Correct	18. けんきゅう	28. にゅういん
9. ちゃわん	19. とうきょう	29. としょかん
10. ひこうき	20. Correct	30. にんぎょう

Writing Exercise (p. 65)

1. Y:「たなかさん、こんにちは。」

   T:「ああ、やまださん、しばらくですね。おげんきですか。」

   Y:「ええ、おかげさまで げんきです。あなたは。」

   T:「ありがとう ございます。わたしも あいかわらずです。」

   Y:「それは けっこうですね。」

2. T:「きょうは いい おてんきですね。がっこうは どうですか。」

   Y:「とても おもしろいです。」

   T:「そうですか。なにが いちばん おもしろいですか。」

   Y:「しんりがくが いちばん おもしろいです。」

   T:「あなたの せんこうは なんですか。」

   Y:「わたしの せんこうは しゃかいがくです。あなたは なんの
   べんきょうを して いますか。」

   T:「わたしの せんこうは まだ きまって いませんが、しょうらい
   かいけいがくの べんきょうを したいと おもって います。」

3. Y:「たなかさん、おはよう　ございます。きのうは　なにを　しましたか。」

　　T:「かいものに　いきました。そして　にほんごの　じびきを　いっさつ
　　　　かいました。あなたは。」

　　Y:「わたしは　かいしゃへ　いきました。そして　しごとを　しました。」

　　T:「あなたの　かいしゃは　じどうしゃの　かいしゃですね。うちから
　　　　とおいですか。」

　　Y:「いいえ、そんなに　とおく　ないです。くるまで
　　　　じゅうごふんぐらいです。」

　　T:「それは　べんりですね。」

APPENDIX B: The Derivation of Hiragana

Both Hiragana and Katakana were derived from Kanji. Hiragana are very abbreviated, cursive forms of Kanji characters, whereas Katakana were formed by selecting particular elements. For example:

Hiragana   Katakana

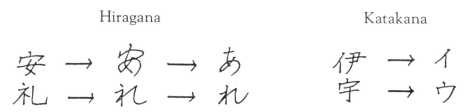

The forty-six basic Hiragana are listed below in their usual order, in vertical rows beginning at the upper right. This is the same as the Hiragana Syllabary on page 12. To the right of each symbol is the Kanji, the Chinese character, from which it was derived.

な 奈	た 太	さ 左	か 加	あ 安
に 仁	ち 知	し 之	き 幾	い 以
ぬ 奴	つ 川	す 寸	く 久	う 宇
ね 祢	て 天	せ 世	け 計	え 衣
の 乃	と 止	そ 曽	こ 己	お 於

わ 和	ら 良	や 也	ま 末	は 波
	り 利		み 美	ひ 比
	る 留	ゆ 由	む 武	ふ 不
	れ 礼		め 女	へ 部
を 袁	ろ 呂	よ 与	も 毛	ほ 保

ん 无	

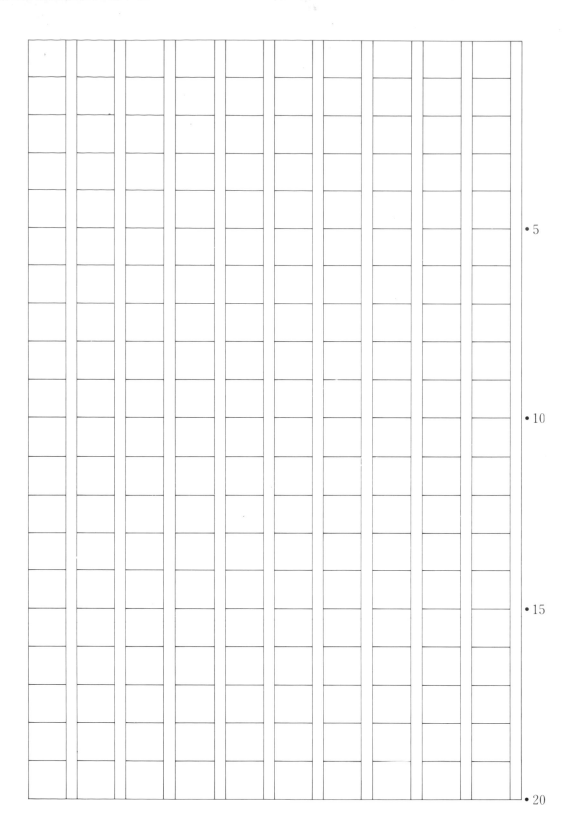

ひらがな   Let's Learn Hiragana

1985 年 3 月 第 1 刷発行
2003 年 7 月 第19刷発行

著 者   ヤスコ・コサカ・ミタムラ
発行者   畑野文夫
発行所   講談社インターナショナル株式会社
         〒112-8652 東京都文京区音羽 1-17-14
         電話 03-3944-6493 （編集部）
               03-3944-6492 （営業部・業務部）
         ホームページ www.kodansha-intl.co.jp

印刷所   大日本印刷株式会社
製本所   大日本印刷株式会社